Womb Wisdom

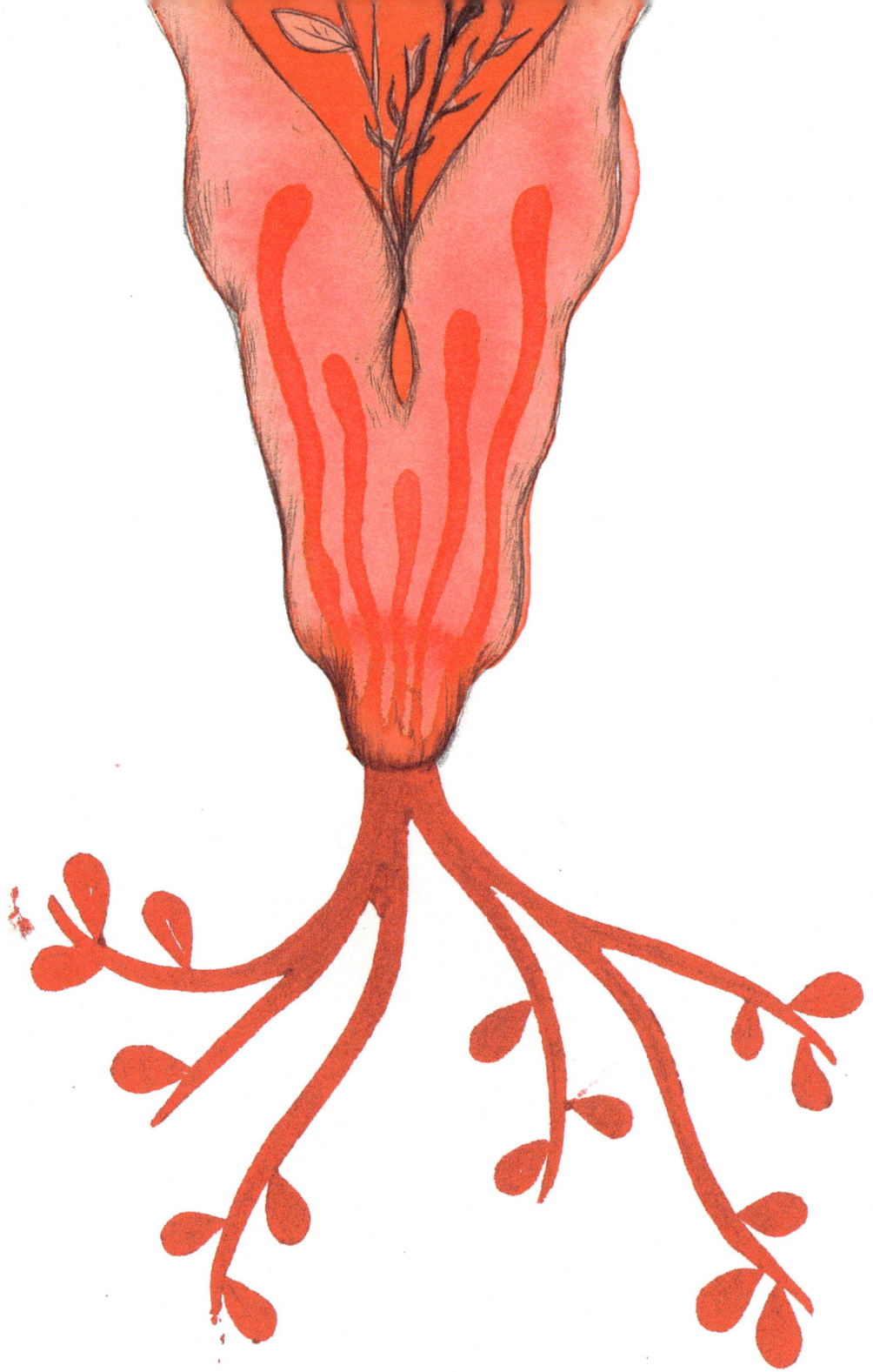

FROM GIRL TO GODDESS

How one woman learned to follow the intuition of her womb

Matador
9 Priory Business Park,
Wistow Road, Kibworth Beauchamp,
Leicestershire. LE8 0RX
Tel: 0116 279 2299
Email: books@troubador.co.uk
Web: www.troubador.co.uk/matador
Twitter: @matadorbooks

ISBN 978 1838594 619

British Library Cataloguing in Publication Data.
A catalogue record for this book is available from the British Library.

Printed and bound by CPI Group (UK) Ltd, Croydon, CR0 4YY

Matador is an imprint of Troubador Publishing Ltd

FSC
www.fsc.org
MIX
Paper from
responsible sources
FSC® C013604

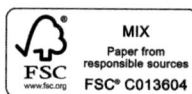

Dedication

This book is dedicated to the fifteen brave women who took a soul-deep journey with me on the Womb Wisdom retreat in Portugal.

Deep inside our wombs we discovered our love, wounding and potential.

MAY ALL WOMEN BE FREE TO
BE THEMSELVES!

CONTENTS

Being a Woman

Slut! Bitch! Freak! Whore!

Yet, I'm still the one that they adore.

Lover, fighter: strong salty tears,

Bears the wounds of years and years.

Witch, temptress, she'll put you under a spell.

Once in her clutches you'll never rebel.

Nag, clean, cook and keep

House and home, stay down – don't leap.

To the bedroom with you!

A saint all day – but at night we play.

Yet, men will never know, how much pleasure,

Down below…

As being a woman – a marvellous thing!

Now, my girl, you can begin!

Breathe Together

Fear holds me closed,
Who could enter?
No one knows.
Find I will and find I must,
The man who I can really trust.

Anger next, what have you done?
How dare assume I would succumb.
Not yours, but mine.
No one to blame,
So I remain,
Autonomous: not yours to claim

Stress, stress – get it done!
STOP! GO! Keep on – RUN!
The list too long,
The day is done,
Never remember who you've become.
Harmony – it's over,
Completed – so why do I feel depleted?

Sadness too I can feel,
Nobody with me to enjoy the meal.
Alone, myself, me and I.
Yet comes inspiration, if I try.
New life, creative projects birthed,
I can give back to Mother Earth.

And love myself, I'm not alone,
Up high I sit upon the throne.
Amazing.
Beautiful.
Full of mirth.
That's why I'm here on planet Earth.

Childhood

Guilt I feel for what's not real,
Not fair for me,
Your attention to steal.
Voices rising, higher and higher –
Not quiet, not once, they never tire.
Surrounded by noise at every meal,
You could not hear my voice I feel.
So rather than fight against the din,
To eat and eat I did begin.

But love, much love we did express,
Tight as peas within our nest.

My childhood, like yours?
No way, no how…
But still, I'm grateful somehow.
It made me the woman I am today.
And so I'd say,
It was the best.
I wouldn't change it.
No more, no less.

A Message from my Grandma

Dance,
Dance!
Go! Be free!
Just know that always,
You're loved by me!

Blockage Versus Power

What holds me back?
I must unpack.
Bring to mind, a painful time,
When as a girl, I tried to find,
The way to become a woman.

All the men I came across,
Seemed to me to be so lost,
Next for comfort,
I turned to her,
Only to find she, too, a blur.

What I needed, I didn't get,
All my love, was not met.
Not by her, then not by me;
I spiralled deep into insanity.
I lost my voice, I could not speak,
Afraid of judgement, I didn't seek

Outside, I appear so strong,
Yet, inside, I don't belong.
All alone I seem to feel,
Comfort myself at every meal.

Protection from judgement and
rejection,
I closed my soul: no reflection.
Refused to love and let them in.
Chose instead to commit a sin.

Bound in chains of my own making,
Constantly doubting my creating.

What holds me back, now today?
Why can't I just,
come out and play?

Well, I feel the time has come –
Now my dance has just begun!
So creative: I sing, I dance,
I paint and draw,
What man alive could ask for
more?

Kind and strong, yet still gentle,
The sight of me will drive him
mental!

Compassion: is my middle name,
Now, no longer I play your game...
My fire, can simply not be tamed,
As deep within me it has claimed
Its rightful place,
Up, up high,
Floating gently in the sky.

A goddess now,
of epic proportion,
to the wind, I throw all caution.

Wise, successful, dancing free...
I invite you to join with me,
In my circle of positivity!

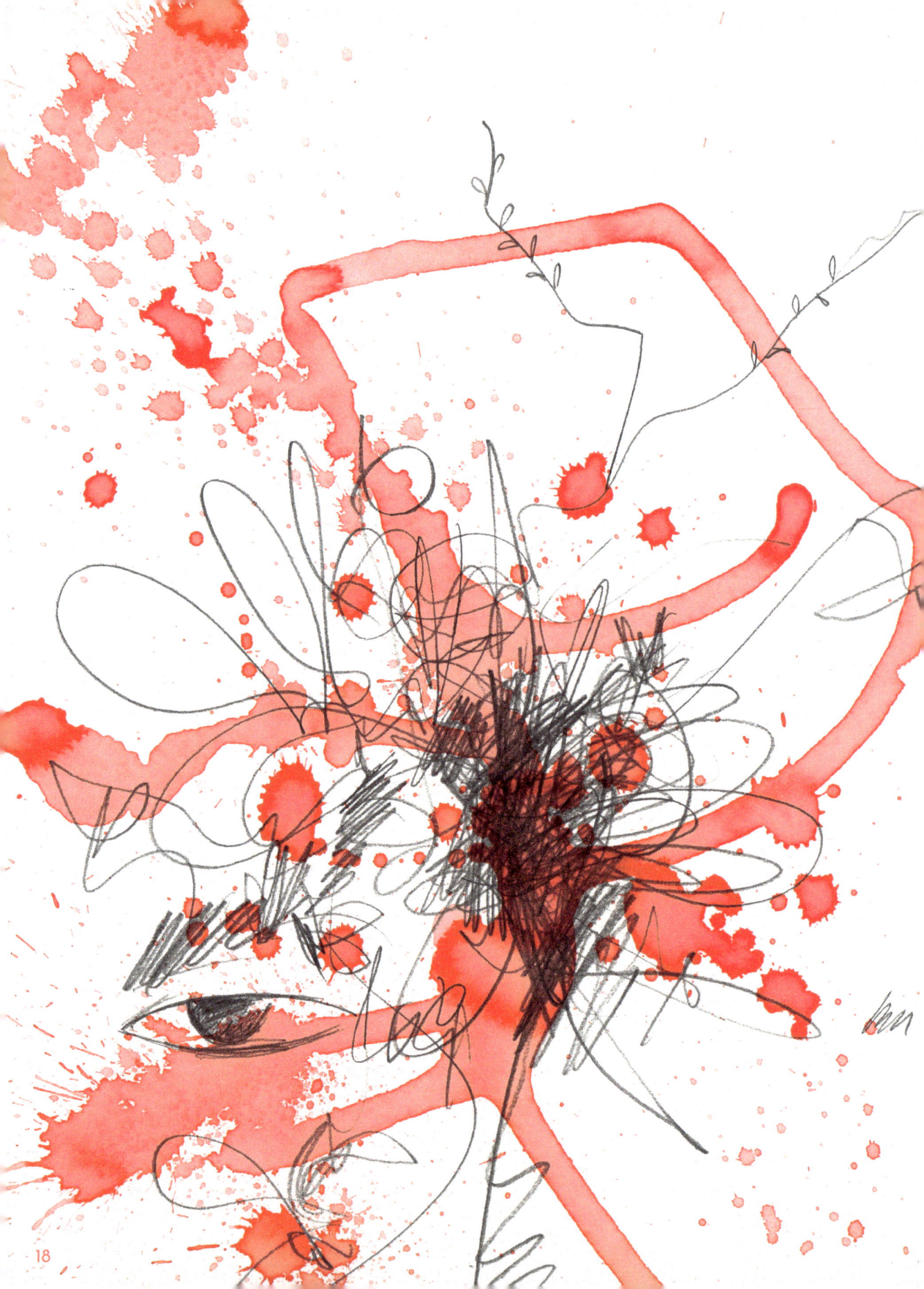

The Clutter of Men

Does anyone know why,
Despite my attempts to try and try,
Men always seem to bring
distraction?
Just when I feel I'm gaining traction.

My interest piqued,
just a fraction,
And – oh yes – my old friend:
attraction.

Deep voice and strength of a
physical kind,
Comes easily to infect my mind,
Stops me flowing gently by,
Starts me thinking: "My, oh my!"

Why is it I cannot be,
Centred on myself – just me?
Now, I suffer from distraction,
I feel I NEED a man for action!
But the truth for all to know,
Is that he needs me, to grow.
Stronger, when we stand together.
Women, men or... whoever!

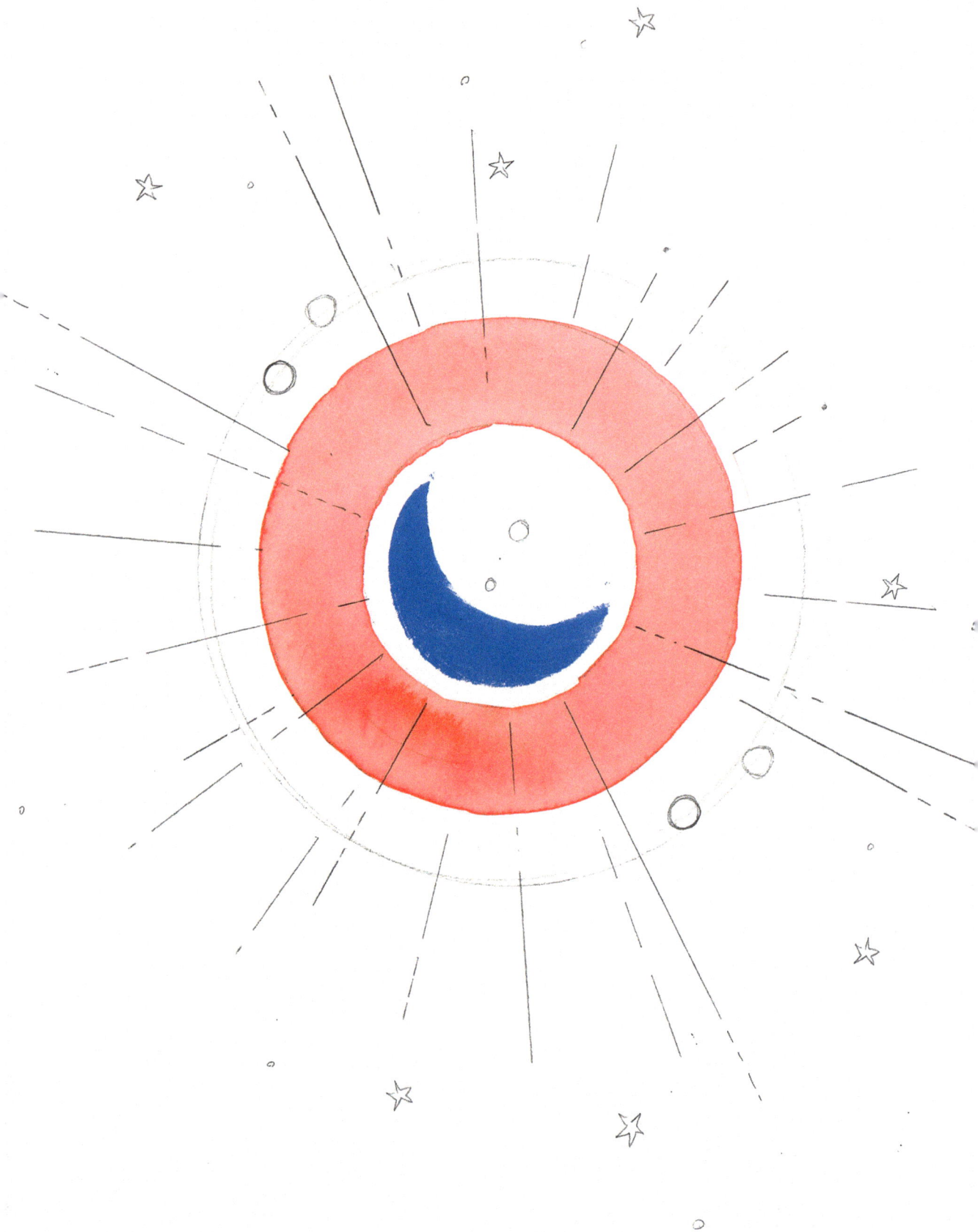

Connection

I danced in your eyes without knowing who you were,
I breathed in your soul without any kind of goal,
You taught me to see just what you see,
I felt validated; loved, little-old-me.
The sun rises and sets and time goes on.
I won't see you again,
From my life you are gone.
But I'll remember your words,
Your caresses and hugs.
We were so warm like bugs in a rug.
You said it; you meant it.
At that moment in time we breathed in;
we were together: neither wanted it to end.

But movement goes on and the world
changes in the wind.

That moment I'll keep in my treasure box,
To remember for times when I feel lost.
I'm a goddess you see and you saw,
I'm perfect as I am – accept any flaw.
I'm hopeful now for MY future,
So powerful, full of love… beaming out.
Sensuality made me feel wild, hot, so full.
An attractive proposition,
Full of possibility…

Mildred isn't Meghan

Outside I sat in the cold,
Minute by minute lost my resolve.
Bouncing around I had been;
Feeling like a juicy queen.
Moment by moment, life was drained.
Minute by minute, love was blamed.
Over and over in my mind,
Memories surfaced, a painful kind.
Not good enough to be
A priority: little-old-me.

The contrast, far, far too vast:
My expectations; what came to pass.
From an embodied intimate space,
To Kings Cross – what a disgrace!
The fear I felt on their faces,
Fallen from all airs and graces.
Deep into despair and loss,
Pissed off with life: simply cross.

I wanted to crawl into his arms,
Show him all my hidden charms.
I needed him to make me safe,
Wrapped up in a full embrace.
Instead, I drowned in my anger,
Whirls and swirls, the same old clangour:
Not good enough: a bit too rough.

Disappointed by you, and then by me,
The pedestal I'd built for thee:
Up, up high upon a throne,
I'd placed my king; I hadn't known.
Supposing myself a queen to be,
Living inside my dream I'd see…

I thought this time it could be different.

But no, not yet.

Insignificant.

I Wonder

I wonder what I could see,
If I simply let myself be.
I wonder what I would find,
If I looked inside my anxious mind.
I wonder what you could be,
If you only let me see.
I wonder what you would find,
If you opened up your beautiful mind.
I wonder when you'll start to trust?
You know the answers – you simply must!
Listen to your heart, my girl,
You'll find inside just so much love.
LOVE! LOVE! LOVE!

Is it WRONG?

Is it wrong that I want to feel you close?
Is it wrong that I want to hear your breath?
Is it wrong that I want to see your eyes?
Is it wrong that I want to taste your mouth?
Is it wrong that I want to smell your scent?
Is it wrong that I don't care if I see you once or
one-thousand times?

This moment in your arms is all I desire.

Is it wrong?

Who am I?

Am I The Judge – who tells you what to do?
Or am I The Lover – who says it's only you?
Am I The Homemaker in her happy home?
Or am I The Rebel – always on her phone?
Am I The Good Girl – always pleasing you?
Or am I The Charmer – who looks good on you?

Does it really matter, who we pretend we are?
Isn't it more important to be true to our bizarre?

Now, just stop pretending to be somebody else.
Now, just show the world your SHINING, BEAUTIFUL SELF!

Shame

I'm sorry I did it,
I couldn't be,
The paragon you wanted to see.

I'm sorry I said it,
I couldn't keep my big mouth shut!

I'm sorry I'm not good enough for you –
I had no idea what I was supposed to do!

I'm sorry you heard me, when I was free.
But now, perhaps, you understand me?

Womb Wisdom

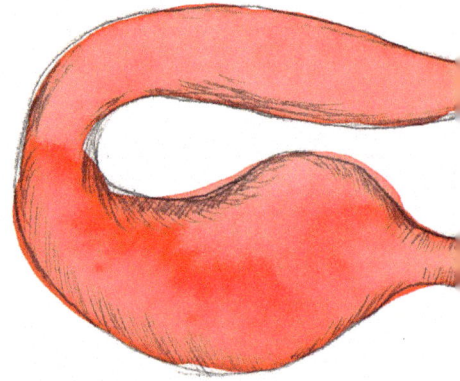

Womb Wisdom, you have it deep inside.
Womb Wisdom, you feel it – as high as the tide.
Womb Wisdom, you know it – from way back when.
Womb Wisdom, just use it on all the men!
Womb Wisdom, intuition from deep down low,
Womb Wisdom, you move it – just go slow.
Womb Wisdom, you'll love it – I'll show you how.
Womb Wisdom, you need it – so much more now.
Womb Wisdom is held by all us girls.
Womb Wisdom, been in us since our hair curled.
Womb Wisdom, the weapon of the feminine queen.
Womb Wisdom, just remember where you've been.

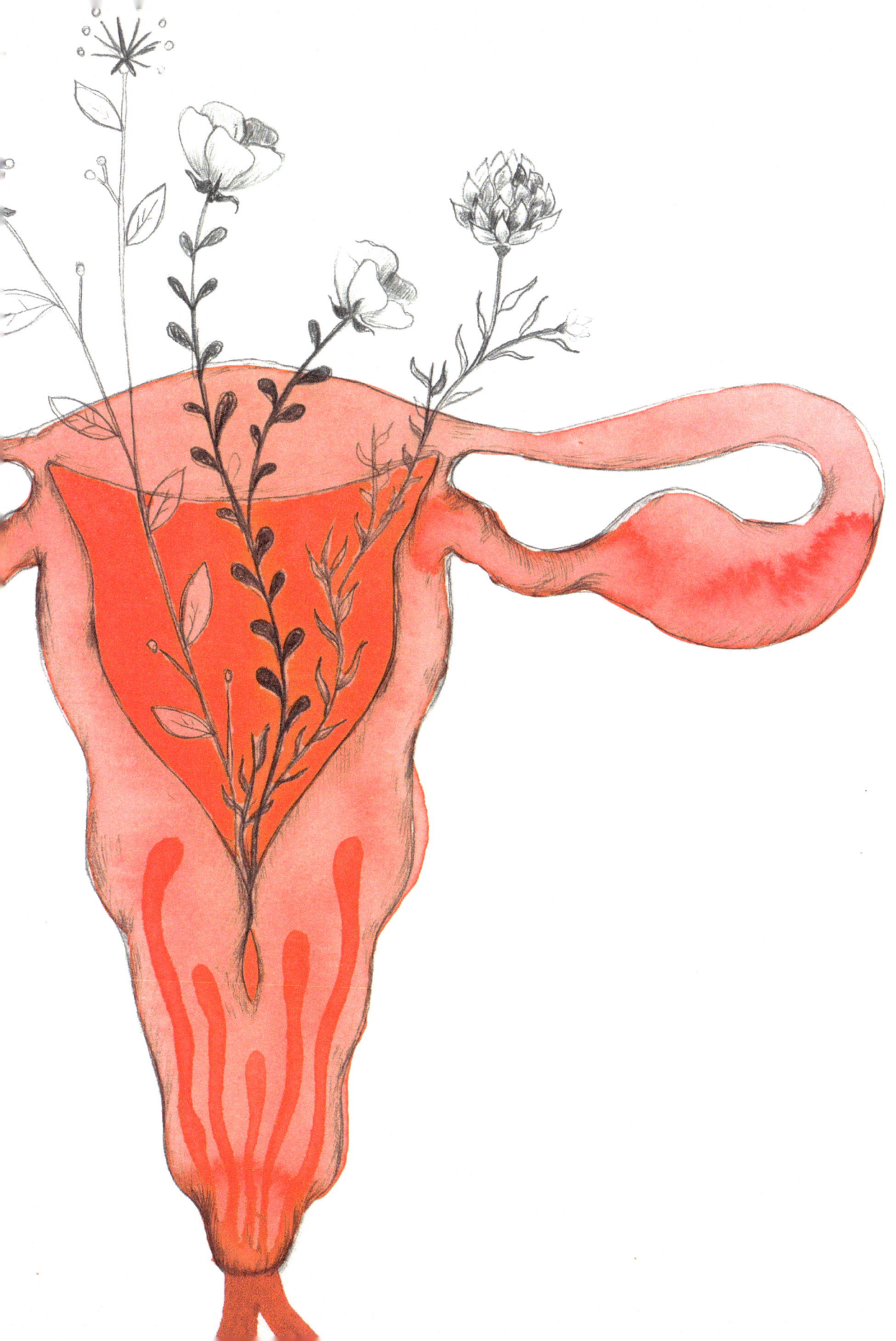

Meditation Quiet

Try to stop thinking.
Keep that mind quiet.
Don't worry where the kids are or what's in your diet.
Hush your busy mind now,
Forget and just release…

Who is that snoring?
Breaking up the peace.
Is she really looking somewhere over there?
Try to stop the thinking,
Don't even care.
Deep breath!
Going inside…
Deep breath!
Coming out.

Try this conscious breathing,
Open up your mouth.
Now you start to feel it,
Coming from up there,
Now you start to love it,
Flicking round your hair.

Moving left to right now,
Circles from your hips.
Moving right to left now,
Taking breath in sips.
Visualise the light now,
Coming from your star.
Heal your body right now,
Sing that mantra 'Ma!'
What did you forget now?
Seems you really are –
Meditating quiet...

Now...

Where did I park my car?

Open your Hips

Open your hips –
Twirls and dips.
Open your thighs –
My! Oh mys!
Open your womb space –
Flow with grace.
Open your soul –
To the deepest goal.
Move like a WOMAN, move like a snake.
Circle and circle – bum in the air,
Don't worry what you look like,
Don't even care!
You're finding your way home now –
Welcome back inside!
You've always known – you were your own guide.

Now, follow your intuition,
Listen to your core –
She's the little child, begging you for more.
Move all your emotions –
Out through those hips.
Squirm and writhe like a snake on a trip.
That's how you do it, and now you feel the score.
Let yourself reach it – just a little more.

Now you feel a WOMAN
'Cause that's what you are.
Now you're really feminine,
A Goddess with a scar.

But nobody can see it, when you hide below,
Wonder how much slower, slower you can go?
Try to really feel it, let your emotions flow…
It's the only way to move it – you have to let it go!
Moving gently through it, like a feather in the breeze –
Sometimes it's more violent – an abrupt sneeze.
But you gotta let yourself feel it,
if you wanna go up high.
The lows are just as valuable – let out a sigh.

Move more freely – however it feels good!
Now you're so ready to come out from your hood.

Let's see your pretty face now: make-up free.
Let's see your lovely smile now; just let it be!

Sisterhood

Sisters one and sisters three,
Sit in circles till you see,
The powerful woman you want to be —
Living inside you and me.

Summon her from your deepest space,
The future is ours to make!

What's the key to all this stuff?
It's not being strong and tough.
Simply, show yourself more love.

Beautiful, powerful, vulnerable woman,
Open here for all to see.
Don't worry about the others, just BE!

And when you open up your soul,
You'll find within a deeper goal.
A space that's open to receive,
More love from her,
From you,
To me.

Take it all, and take it now.
You deserve it — I'll show you how!

Because my dear,
By now you see,
The beautiful goddess you want to be.

Deep down inside, you've always known,
How to sit, upon the throne,
Just lower your tone,
It's time to show,
All the world!
So stop that moan...

Turn it simply into one of pleasure,
No longer need you sit and measure,
For now you know...
Each of us – her time to glow.

Show your sister that you love her,
Bring her out from under cover –
Feel as strong as you can be,
Reflected in love,
For all to see.

Now you hold your hand with me,
And we know that we can be,
Sisters stronger when together –
Stand in circles: we're so clever!

Always have we been – but now,
We see our queen, somehow.
Singing softly, from our core,
Silently, aching out for more.

Who's to know what's in store?
Come with me
– and learn to ROAR!

You Are

You are POWERFUL!
You are SEXY!
You are STRONG!

Why haven't you noticed that you belong?

You are SAFE!
You are LOVED!
You are FREE!

Why can't you simply accept your Me?

You are RHYTHM!
You are LOVE!
You are SOUL!

Why don't you let yourself be whole?

You are BEAUTIFUL!
You are BOUNTIFUL!
You are BLESSED!

Isn't it time you got yourself dressed?

Rebirth

Spiralling, rocking, memories keep knocking,
Fears I had,
A time that was bad.
Was it in this lifetime or from a life that's past?
Happening now or a time that didn't last?
Deep inside the tunnel, stuck in a small space,
Or being chased by a man with a scary face?
I better stay small now, I better try and hide,
Better keep myself now, stuck in my inside.
Am I really safe here in my body on this earth?
Or am I still hiding behind my stomach and its girth?

In Child's Pose my patience grows
Ever shorter – I am my father's daughter!
My legs won't bend, when will it end?
Bending over just isn't my friend!

I am safe. I belong. I am held.
Breathe just a little; let it meld.
NOW, it is the time for my rebirth.
Time for me to fill up, with bubbles of pure mirth!
Breathe in the light now, share with Mother Earth.
Relax into love now, remembering your birth!

Reflected Back to Me

I've considered my behaviour,
I thought about it too.
I think I might have realised –
Myself I found in you.

I thought it was all your fault,
Thought you were to blame,
Now I think I found out,
I had to learn from the game.

I thought you did it to me,
as innocent as I cry.
But now I'm starting to see it –
as clear as time goes by.

It's reflected back to me now,
the lesson I must learn.
It's becoming awful clear now,
Time to take my turn.
And get inside my head now –
See what I create,
More problems than friends now,
It seems I replicate...

But what can I change now?
I know my pattern well.

Deepen my awareness,
Ring the alarm bell!
Now, I spot my trigger,
Before the pattern came.
Now, I assess if I really need
the pain?
Or have I finally learnt,
The way to win the game?

Let it all go now!
I'm the only one to blame.
Reflected back to me now:
What I put in, I get out.

Keep my vibration high now:
Raise what I expect.
Manifest my dreams now:
Create what I desire.
Use my talents wisely:
Of this I never tire.
A beautiful reflection of
What I really need,
Coming back to me now...

Just as I decreed.

Bending like a Banana

I found that very difficult,
I think you did as well,
In fact at times we thought,
We were going through living hell.

The teacher told us to bend now,
A place I don't know where,
But all we felt was pain there,
Like falling down a stair.

You've got to try to breathe through it –
In nose and out mouth,
I'm feeling very stupid: the only one
who can't work it out.
I want to scream and shout now –
Why is it only me?

Surely, I'm not the only one –
An acrobat cannot be?

But, now we sit up together,
I look around the room,
The smiling faces tell me,
We all suffered the same doom.

I know I'm just like you now,
the same we can just be.
Feeling under-flexible –
You're just as bad as me!

Now we have shown up,
Doing the work for ourselves.

Now we know we're stronger,
When deep inside we delve.
You and me together –
A team until the end.

Maybe tomorrow,
We all will learn to bend?

Acceptance

Learn to accept the spiders, learn to love the food –
pretty soon you'll realise you're actually in a good mood.

Take time for yourself: it's what you came here to do.
Even if you never imagined, a loo with a scenic view.

Go swim in the river, it's cold but exhilarating too,
even wash your hair, with the lush conditioner you threw.

Enter into the dome, take a breath or moan,
Move your body slowly, sigh, yawn; groan.

Shake it all off now, move energy out the way,
Take a breath of lion or a dragon on its day.

Purge out all the energy: negative doesn't need you.
Feel yourself lighter, sing like Peggy-Sue.

Lie down in shavasana, deeper breaths for you,
In nose out of mouth,
Sink into the floor and stick to it like glue.

Now, it's almost over. Check-in: How'd you do?
Were you really feeling it: what's moving in you?

Listen to your Tribe now, it resonates with you.
Feeling all the same now, you know what I've been through.

Thank you to my Teacher, for showing me the way,
Thank you to the Earth for letting me live this day!

It's All Welcome Here

You said it's all welcome,
You told me not to care.
But I can't help feeling embarassed,
when wind flows from under there!

You told me not to worry,
If I let out a little burp.
But I still want to scurry,
And feel quite a twerp.

You screamed it wasn't supposed to be pretty –
When I was shaking my arse,
But I can't help thinking –
I'm shaking out a fart!

You said relax your jaw –
Breathe a little more,
But I'm still holding on now
To the girl without a flaw.

You said welcome deeper breaths now,
From deep inside your core.
But I can't help feeling stuck now,
Worshipping the floor.

You said I would feel better,
If I just felt through all of it,
But now all my emotions have sent me
Spiralling down the pit.

You said let it out now,
It's the only thing to do…

You actually were right though –
I should have believed in you!

Awakening from the Spell

A couple of things have come to me,
things I know only too well.
It seems for the last 20 years I've been put under a spell.
The spell it dragged me under,
Told me I wasn't enough,
And now I'm doing all the work – I find I'm really tough!

They told me I was stupid, they told me I was fat.
I should have screamed,
"Look at yourself! You self-projecting twat!"
They said I wasn't as tall as her or even quite as nice.
I should have told them to shut up, not only once but
twice!

But I didn't take that path as I was just a little girl.
Instead I chose to eat and eat and make my hair curl,
I thought if I was quiet then nobody could see,
I tried to bury all my light deep under a tree.

I didn't speak for years and years in case I got it wrong,
Only now I'm really realising I have a beautiful song.
It seems I'm rather better than I thought I could be –
Even writing poetry for all the world to see!
I am aware now of my patterns,
behaviours and triggers, all three.

Now, I'm just discovering who I really want to be.
A teacher, an artist or maybe even a mum?
Now it seems the real journey has only just begun,
You see I'm nearly 40, time is marching on.
I feel my clock is ticking – I haven't got that long.
But all my parents' friends say that
I'm still really just so young:
My whole life in front of me…
Bumbling along.

So I will see what Spirit shows me, the way I have to go.
See how water flows me until I really, really know.
Listen to my intuition: my womb it knows the way.
Sooner or later I'll discover it,
Tomorrow or today.

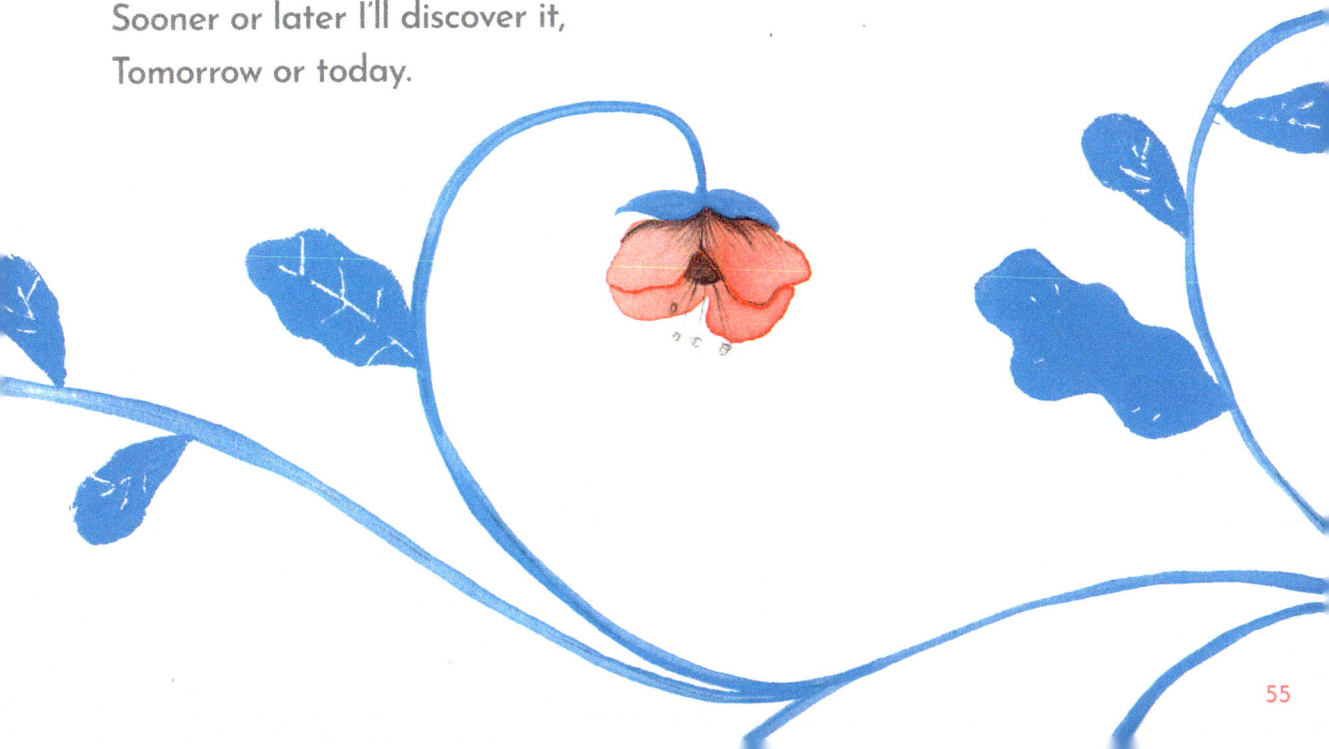

Worthy

I think I will take a shower,
There's nothing else to do.
And then maybe if there's more
time — try'n push out a poo!

I'm told I must be silent,
Speak to no one but you.
So I'm writing in my journal —
Pages one to twenty-two.

You see it's very clear now:
When silent you can hear,
The thoughts inside your womb,
Now becoming loud and clear.

You obviously were not listening,
With all that chatter to do.
Too busy making friends,
And checking I'm like you.

But only when you can't speak,
Does the mind go overdrive,
I wonder why I did that?
I wonder why I lied?

You see it's very simple —
You must listen to your womb,
She's shouting out the answers —
Hoping to avoid the tomb.

You've left her deep below now —
Deep inside your core,
If only you would listen —
She'd throw you to the floor.

You knew it all along though,
You knew it wasn't right.
Should have heeded your vagina,
When she told you it was tight.

So open up your throat now,
You know what you need to say.
Reflecting on your womb space
Has really shown the way.

Tell the world you're good enough —
Just the way you are!
Tell them deep inside you,
You know that you're a star!
Now you must stop hiding
Your light from Mother Earth.
Rather better to share it —
And fill up full of mirth!

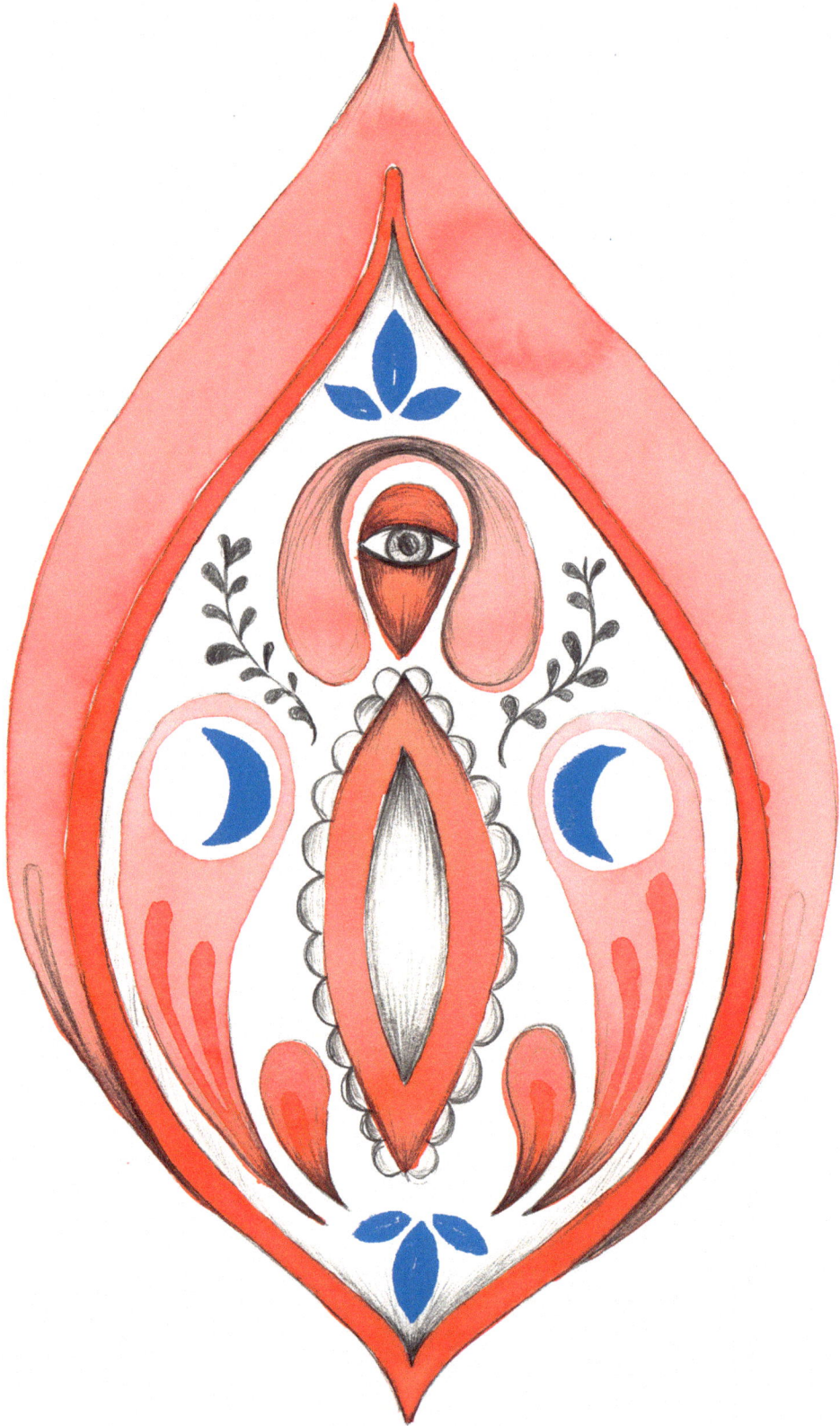

Beautiful

It's not that I haven't enjoyed nature,
But I'm kinda looking forward to
The face pack and the bath that I have planned to do.
A shave; a body scrub — I'll feel good as new!
I know these things are external and just between me and you,
I take this time for me, to stop me feeling blue.

No longer conditioned by magazine hullabaloo.
I know I'm really bountiful: not at all too much.
I know I'm so blissful when I consciously stop the rush.
Finally, I see my beauty: it's my soul, not my body, that counts.
Breathing all the way through it has removed all my doubts.

Procrastination energy has been my daily friend,
But now towards my projects, I will begin to bend.
Untangle all my energy: leave the drama behind,
Reclaim back my power, use the I you declined!

So bleed with me woman, don't make it difficult to be you.
Unconditional love to self, that's what you need to do!

Happy Hippos

As happy as a hippo wallowing in mud.
As beautiful as a flower coming from the blood.
Yay to my belly and how it falls!
Yay to my breasts when I stand tall!
Breathe with me woman – show me feminine love,
See me all over – free as a dove!

Curves so round, undulating unbound!
Women so powerful they ought to be crowned!
So forget the competition and support each other to see,
The beauty I see before me, is reflected back in me!

So what if I'm fat or your boobs are too small?
So what if you can't see what I see?
Revel in yourself – you are exactly where you need to be.
Learn from the experience – flourish for all to see!
Because you only have one life, so you may as well feel it all,
Take in the joy – the rise, the fall,
And rise sister, RISE! Up to who you are.
Realise your magnificence through breathing from your heart!

Take in your fantasticity through your belly of brilliance,
And feel deep into your root – the wonder that you are!

A Journey of Sisters

Burping, farting, screaming and crying,
Any one would think you were dying!
But no, you chose this difficult path,
To help you relax – it's better than a bath!

I've got some issues – I told my friends,
They'd heard it all before – their ears wouldn't bend.
So off to retreat I took myself,
Feeling alone, as small as an elf.

But when I arrived I found them – my Tribe,
Gorgeous Goddesses – the feminine kind.
And in it together, we found ourselves,
Much bigger, in fact, than a drove of elves!

Journeying side by side,
One sister then the next,
Turns out we had more in common
Than we might expect…

Awakening on a journey longer than this piece.
Loving the burning, emotional release.
Sit around the fire, singing out our songs,
Waiting for food, now sounded by a gong!

In it together, each woman side by side,
Not one can remember the last time she really cried,
Or showed the world her real rage:
Releasing Kali from her cage.

No longer the small one, drowning in her fear,
Now she's the woman all want to be near.

Thank you to my sisters, for bringing me here.
Thank you to the women, who supported me to be me!
Thank you to the river, the fire and the tree!

Reveal

Did you really think you could hide it?
Did you really think we wouldn't see?
Thought we wouldn't notice,
The woman you wanted to be?

Did you think you could trick us?
Take us all for fools?
Lead us up the garden path to the perfect you?

Maybe you thought we would judge you?
Maybe you thought we'd say no?
Maybe you'd feel some rejection –
Of the ME you wanted to show?

How do you feel now we've seen the real you?
What do you feel when met with acceptance, love and what's true?

Open up: let yourself feel!

Let us see inside, to where the emotion grew.
Show us you're human — we've felt the same as you.
Too fearful to show it before, in case rejection was due.

So breathe in my acceptance and breathe out your surprise!
Breathe in my adoration and breathe out your resistance.
Breathe in your You and Me you will find.
Breathe out Me and You cannot be denied!

And now?

Just BE.

Love me as I Am

You think I'm confident,
You think I'm strong.
But the truth is, it's the only way I get along.

You think I'm funny? Funny as I fake,
But that's just how I cover up my mistakes.

You think I'm hilarious:
HA! HA! HA!
I make you laugh to cover my scar.

You think I'm beautiful.
Pretty. Little. Me.
If only you saw, the ugly I see.

You think I'm so cool,
But I learnt that in school,
If you want to be popular,
You better fit in:
Eat next to nothing,
Get really thin.

You think I'm so clever – got it all sorted out.
That's because I cover up, with my motormouth.
You think I'm lovely – as nice as can be,
But really I'm as angry as a wasp or a bee.

You think I'm nicer than sweet-cherry-pie,
But I'm more and more a needy mess as time goes by.

You think you can love me, just as I am?
I really hope you can – my magnificent man!

Pure-fact

Pure-fact: truer than true.
This, my friend, is the real you!
Perfect, you must understand,
Is a fallacy, strong and grand,
Nowhere to be found in this land.

Are you pale or are you tanned?
Are you big or are you small?
You should stand even more tall...
STOP! Don't listen to the media call:
"Not pretty enough!"
"A bit too rough!"

Simply start to really see!
What you have to offer the world,
Does not revolve around hair curls!
The beautiful woman you really are,
Is not hidden by that scar.

Laugh loudly, puff out your chest!
It's infectious: you know the rest!

Breathe the freshest air into your lungs,
Smile, and see what becomes...

When girls believe in themselves –
They grow into WOMEN.